Copyright © 2024 Emerson J. Dias

All rights reserved

No part of this book may be reproduced, or stored in a retrieval system, or transmitted in any form or by any means, electronic, mechanical, photocopying, recording, or otherwise, without express written permission of the publisher.

I0515192

CONTENTS

Copyright
Introduction — 2
Chapter 1: The Greatness of Babylon - Building an Empire — 4
Chapter 2: Economy and Trade in Babylon - The Roots of Prosperity — 8
Chapter 3: The Wealth of Knowledge - Babylon as a Centre of Innovation — 16
Chapter 4: Leadership and Governance - The Code of Hammurabi and Justice — 21
Chapter 5: The Role of Religion and Spirituality in Babylon — 27
Chapter 6: The Art of Diplomacy and Foreign Relations — 35
Chapter 7: Legacy and Fall - The Lessons of Babylon's Decline — 43
Chapter 8: The Secret of Babylon's Riches - Modern Applications — 50
Conclusion — 57
Appendix to "The Secrets of Babylon" — 60
Final considerations — 64

EMERSON J. DIAS

The Secrets of Babylon

Lessons in Wealth and Prosperity from the Ancient Empire

Emerson J. Dias

INTRODUCTION

*Exploring the Wealth and
Wisdom of Babylon*

Imagine an ancient empire, born between rivers, whose name echoes to this day. Babylon, with its hanging gardens, imposing walls and visionary leaders, was more than a prosperous civilisation. It was a symbol of power, wealth and innovation. But Babylon's true greatness was not limited to its imposing buildings or its military conquests. It lay in the practical wisdom that its leaders and citizens applied day after day, in the laws that established order and justice, and in the innovations that transformed a simple piece of land into the beating heart of the ancient economy.

In this book, we will explore not only what made Babylon one of the greatest powers of antiquity, but how these secrets of prosperity can be applied to our modern lives. The lessons learnt over the millennia, forged in the heat of the Mesopotamian desert, still resonate strongly in the 21st century. Babylon teaches us that success - be it personal, financial or professional - is built on strategy, innovation and visionary leadership.

Throughout this book, you will be guided through fascinating stories about the building of the Babylonian empire and the pillars that sustained it. Each chapter offers a combination of theory and practice, allowing you to apply these lessons in a real and tangible way in your everyday life. You'll discover that just as the Babylonians overcame challenges and thrived amid adversity, you too can build your own journey of success and growth.

This book is designed to be a guide, a practical tool for those seeking to understand how the secrets of Babylon can impact their own lives. It's not just about history, it's about action. Combining practical advice, exercises and reflections, you will learn to develop a clear vision of your goals, to plan strategically and to lead with wisdom and purpose.

CHAPTER 1: THE GREATNESS OF BABYLON - BUILDING AN EMPIRE

"Every greatness you see today was once a distant dream." This is a timeless truth, and no civilisation exemplifies this better than Babylon. When we look at the history of this majestic empire, we are reminded of the power of strategic planning and long-term vision. But what can we learn in a practical way from the rise of one of the most extraordinary cities of antiquity?

Historical context: The emergence of a power

Babylon, located between the Tigris and Euphrates rivers in what is now Iraq, emerged as a city-state at the beginning of the second millennium BC. Despite its modest beginnings, the city quickly stood out for its strategic location and rich culture. *It wasn't just the geography that favoured Babylon, but the mentality of its leaders.* Every decision made was aimed at taking the city to the next level. This ambitious spirit was evident during the reign of Hammurabi, Babylon's first great king, who expanded the empire and unified Mesopotamia.

However, it was under Nebuchadnezzar II, centuries later, that Babylon reached the height of its glory. Known for his military conquests and especially for his building skills, Nebuchadnezzar transformed the city into a symbol of power and beauty.

Curiosity: The impact of Nebuchadnezzar II

Nebuchadnezzar II was not only a formidable military leader; he was also a visionary when it came to architecture and urban development. Under his command, Babylon became famous for its grandiose walls and majestic buildings, such as the Temple of Marduk. *One of the greatest architectural wonders attributed to this period is the Hanging Gardens of Babylon, one of the Seven Wonders of the Ancient World.* These gardens, supposedly built as a gift for his wife, Amitis, were a veritable oasis in the desert, a metaphor for the empire itself, which flourished in the midst of adversity.

But more than a symbol of wealth, the Hanging Gardens and the walls of Babylon demonstrate Nebuchadnezzar's commitment to a long-term vision. He knew that in order to guarantee the empire's durability and success, *he needed more than military conquests; he needed to create something that would last for centuries.* And that's exactly what he did.

Practical Lesson: Vision and Strategic Planning

Now, stop for a moment and think: how can you apply this visionary mindset to your own life or business? Often, we get so caught up in everyday tasks that we forget to look to the future. However, just as Nebuchadnezzar built Babylon with a clear vision, you too can design your success from a solid, well-defined plan.

Think of Babylon as a living example of strategic planning. The city didn't become a powerhouse overnight; every brick was laid with a purpose. *That's the key: having a clear purpose in everything you do.* But how do you turn this philosophy into something tangible and applicable?

Steps to develop your long-term vision:

1. **Define your end goal**
   Just as Nebuchadnezzar had in mind to turn Babylon into the most splendid city in the world, you too must have a clear destination. *Where do you want to be in 10,*

15 or 20 years' time? That's the starting point for any successful plan.

2. **Break it down into smaller goals**
   Build your "Babylon" little by little. What can you do this year, or even this month, that will bring you closer to your ultimate goal? *Smaller goals make the path less intimidating and easier to follow.*

3. **Stay flexible**
   Even the great Babylonian empire faced challenges and setbacks. The important thing is not to give up in the face of difficulties, but to *adapt and adjust your plan* as necessary. Having a long-term vision doesn't mean blindly following a route without considering changes along the way.

4. **Surround yourself with the right tools**
   Nebuchadnezzar had the best architects, engineers and strategists. Who are the "tools" you need to build your empire? *Seek out knowledge, mentors and alliances that will help you achieve your goal.*

Practical exercise: Planning your own empire

Just as Nebuchadnezzar had a clear vision and followed it, now is the time for you to think about your own long-term plans. Grab pen and paper (or your favourite digital device) and follow the steps below to draw up a life or business plan inspired by Babylon's grandeur.

1. **Write down your long-term vision**:
   Think about where you want to be in 10 years. Describe what your life, your work, your relationships and your health will be like. *The clearer and more detailed your vision, the better you'll be able to achieve it.*

2. **Break this vision down into 5-year goals**:
   What milestones do you need to achieve in the next five years to reach your 10-year vision? *This will make your*

plan more concrete and realisable.

3. **Create an annual plan**:
   What can you do in the next year to start this journey? *Think of practical, tangible actions.* This will be your initial "brick" in building your personal empire.

4. **Re-evaluate and adjust regularly**:
   Just as an architect reviews his building plans, you should also review your life plan regularly. *This will allow you to make the necessary adjustments and stay on track.*

The Power of Persistence

Perhaps one of the most important lessons we can learn from Babylon is persistence. *No empire is built overnight.* Just as the walls of Babylon were built with patience and determination, so should your journey towards success.

Nebuchadnezzar didn't give up in the face of challenges, and neither should you. Difficulties will come, setbacks are inevitable, but just as Babylon became an icon of greatness, your vision of the future can also be realised, as long as you are willing to build, one brick at a time, with focus and determination.

Now is the time to start building your own "Babylon". With the right tools, *there are no limits to what you can achieve.*

CHAPTER 2: ECONOMY AND TRADE IN BABYLON - THE ROOTS OF PROSPERITY

"Where there is trade, there is growth, and where there is growth, there is power." Babylon didn't become an imposing empire just because of its military strength or its magnificent buildings. Its real power lay in its trade routes and a well-regulated economy. Babylon's prosperity was built on the ability to connect East and West, to create networks for the exchange of goods, ideas and cultures, and to maintain all this with a solid and fair financial structure.

Economic fundamentals: The commercial heart of Babylon

Located between the Tigris and the Euphrates, Babylon was strategically positioned to become the central point of the trade routes linking eastern and western civilisations. Babylonian merchants were adept at trading goods such as grain, textiles, precious metals and spices, and quickly realised the importance of controlling trade routes.

But what really set Babylon apart from other civilisations was not just its geographical location. *It was the way they structured their economy and the fairness with which they handled their transactions.* Trade flourished because there were clear regulations to ensure that all parties involved in a negotiation were safe and treated fairly. Trade was therefore more than just an exchange of goods - it was the foundation of a network of trust.

This network of trust expanded not only within Babylon, but also between other civilisations. Babylon was a link between Egypt, India and China, connecting products and cultures in a way that other regions simply could not. *The secret of Babylonian prosperity lay in its ability to build bridges between distant worlds, both literally and figuratively.*

Curiosity: The Code of Hammurabi as a tool for economic regulation

One of the most fascinating curiosities about Babylon is the fact that its famous Code of Hammurabi was not only limited to criminal matters, but also regulated commercial activities. *The Code of Hammurabi, dating from around 1754 BC, is one of the oldest collections of laws in history, and was crucial in guaranteeing the stability and prosperity of Babylonian commerce.*

Hammurabi, one of Babylon's most important kings, understood that for an economy to grow sustainably, it needed to be regulated fairly. For example, the Code established clear rules on how commercial contracts should be made, how the prices of goods and services were determined, and what punishments would be applied in the event of fraud or failure to honour agreements. *These regulations gave traders confidence that their transactions would be protected and that there would be mechanisms to resolve disputes.*

Imagine how difficult it would be to do business in a society where you can't trust contracts or where the rules change from one day to the next. That's why Babylon flourished - the rules were clear, and that encouraged growth and stability.

Practical lesson: The importance of a regulated economy

Now, how can you apply this historical knowledge to your personal life or your business? The answer lies in the importance of having a solid, fair and transparent structure for your finances. *Just as the Code of Hammurabi was fundamental to Babylon's economic success, establishing clear rules for your financial management could be what you need to achieve prosperity.*

Have you ever stopped to think that what often prevents personal or business financial success is not a lack of resources, but a lack of organisation and fair principles to guide your transactions? *When your finances are clear, organised and based on solid rules, you create an environment of trust and stability that facilitates growth.*

Steps to building solid financial management

Managing your finances effectively is fundamental to building a financially stable and prosperous life. Just as Babylon prospered by establishing clear and fair rules for trade, it is crucial that you create your own financial "laws" to ensure that your goals are consistently achieved. Below, we'll detail the steps to building solid financial management, which will not only help organise your finances, but also enable long-term growth.

1. Define your financial rules

The first step to controlling your finances is to define your own rules, i.e. your financial "laws".

Just as the Code of Hammurabi provided a clear framework for business transactions in Babylon, you need to define the boundaries and guidelines that will govern your money. These rules may vary from person to person, but the basic principle is to ensure that you have a clear vision of your finances and that everything you do is aligned with your goals.

Here are some essential questions to help you define your financial rules:

- **What is your spending limit?** Knowing how much you can spend each month without jeopardising your financial goals is essential. It prevents you from spending beyond your means and helps you maintain a financial balance.
- **How do you manage your savings?** *Are you saving part of what you earn or does everything that comes in end up being spent?* Set a clear rule about how much you should save each month, whether for emergencies or to invest in your future dreams.
- **What are your financial priorities?** Your financial rules should reflect your priorities. If your goal is to buy a house, for example, part of your monthly budget should be earmarked for this. If your priority is to pay off debts, this will be the main focus of your finances.

These rules create a framework that guides your daily financial decisions. Without these guidelines, it's easy to lose control and make impulsive decisions that can jeopardise your financial progress.

2. Create a realistic budget

Your budget is the "empire" you are building financially. Think of it as the foundation on which everything else will be built.

Many people associate the word "budget" with something restrictive, but it's actually the opposite. A well-made budget gives you freedom, because you know exactly what you can spend and what you have to save. This eliminates the anxiety of overspending or not having enough at the end of the month.

Here are some steps to create an efficient budget:
- **List all your income and expenditure**. This includes your fixed income (salary, rent, etc.) and your fixed expenses (rent, bills, groceries). *Make sure you are realistic and detailed with your spending, including small expenses that, when accumulated, can weigh you down at the end of the month.*
- **Categorise your expenses into essential and non-essential**. Essential expenses are those you can't avoid

(housing, food, bills). Non-essentials are the extras (entertainment, restaurants, shopping). *By identifying your non-essential expenses, you can make adjustments and cut back where necessary.*

- **Set monthly savings targets**. *A good rule of thumb is to save at least 20 per cent of your income.* If that seems like a lot, start with less, but make saving a priority. As your finances improve, you can increase this percentage.
- **Stick to your budget**. The secret to financial success lies not in creating a perfect budget, but in following it consistently. There's no point in having a plan if you don't use it in your day-to-day life. The ideal is to review your budget periodically to ensure that it is still in line with your objectives.

3. Build a support network

Babylon's prosperity did not depend on a single merchant or city, but on a vast network of trade routes and partners. In the same way, to achieve financial stability, you need to build a support network.

This network may include:

- **Financial mentors**. A mentor is someone who has already travelled the financial path you want to follow and can share valuable advice. *This could be a financial adviser or someone in your network who has experience in financial management.*
- **Financial tools**. Today, there are many apps and tools that help you manage your finances in a practical and automated way. *From apps that monitor your spending to personalised financial spreadsheets, these tools help you keep track of your income and expenses in an organised way.*
- **Business partnerships**. If you have a business, building strategic alliances can be essential to your financial growth. *Just as the Babylonians created trade routes to expand their economy, you can build partnerships that increase your opportunities and profits.*

Remember that financial success doesn't happen in a vacuum. The more support and resources you have around you, the greater your ability to make smart decisions and achieve your goals more quickly.

4. Maintain transparency in all your transactions

The Code of Hammurabi teaches one of the most valuable lessons about finance: the importance of transparency. It established clear rules on how business transactions should be carried out, ensuring that all parties involved were treated fairly.

In your financial life, transparency means:

- **Be honest with your accounts**. *Don't "make up" your expenses or income.* Have a clear picture of how much you really spend and earn. This avoids unpleasant surprises and allows you to make better financial decisions.
- **Avoid hidden debts**. Some debts can go unnoticed if you don't monitor them. Take full control of all your financial obligations, from loans to credit cards. *Make sure you're not neglecting any debts that could jeopardise your finances in the future.*
- **Be clear about your business**. If you're an entrepreneur or work with freelancers, be transparent about prices, deadlines and expectations. This builds trust with your clients and partners, creating a reputation for reliability, which is essential for long-term growth.

Practical exercise: Develop your financial management plan

Now that you have an overview of the principles for building sound financial management, it's time to put this knowledge into practice. By following the steps below, you can create a personal or business financial management plan based on the principles of fairness, transparency and organisation.

1. **Assess your current financial situation**
    - Make a detailed list of your **assets** (what you own), **liabilities** (your debts) and **monthly income**.
    - *Clarity is the first step to making good financial decisions.* Knowing exactly where you stand

financially allows you to make decisions based on real data, not assumptions.

2. **Set your financial goals**
   - Think about what you want to achieve financially in the next five to ten years.
   - *It could be paying off a debt, saving for a big investment or expanding your business.* Setting clear goals makes planning easier and motivates financial discipline.

3. **Create a budget**
   - Based on your financial assessment and your goals, create a budget that takes into account your essential expenses, savings and investments.
   - *This is your personal "Code of Hammurabi".* It will guide your finances, helping you to prioritise what's really important.

4. **Monitor and adjust your plan regularly**
   - It's not enough to create a financial plan. *You need to review it regularly to make sure you're still on track.*
   - Just as the Babylonian traders adapted their routes and strategies, you must be flexible and adjust your plan as necessary, ensuring that it remains relevant and effective.

Building solid financial management is the way to achieve not only stability, but also financial freedom. *With planning, discipline and transparency, you can transform your finances and build a prosperous future.*

The power of regulation

Babylon teaches us that prosperity is not the result of chance. *It is the result of careful planning, clear rules and a network of trust.* In a world where transactions were regulated by a fair code, Babylon became an economic powerhouse that lasted for centuries.

In the same way, you can build your own prosperity, whether in your personal life or in your business, by following principles of fairness, organisation and transparency. By adopting these practices, *you will not only create a solid foundation for success, but you will also be building a financial "Babylon" that can stand the test of time.*

CHAPTER 3: THE WEALTH OF KNOWLEDGE - BABYLON AS A CENTRE OF INNOVATION

"The true power of a civilisation lies in its knowledge, and Babylon was a giant in this respect."

Babylon was not only an economic or military centre, but also a veritable cradle of innovation, education and science. The knowledge produced by this ancient civilisation not only shaped the immediate future of its inhabitants, but also echoed for generations, influencing cultures and nations far beyond its borders. What the Babylonians developed in the areas of mathematics, astronomy and cuneiform writing served as the basis for the progress of the civilisations that followed.

As we explore the history of Babylon, we see that its wealth of knowledge was, in fact, the foundation of its greatness. *And just as the Babylonians prospered through the relentless pursuit of learning and innovation, we too can apply these principles to transform our own lives.*

Education and Science in Babylon

Imagine a time when knowledge wasn't just a click away. *Yet the Babylonians managed to create complex systems that revolutionised the way we live today.* They were masters of maths, astronomy and developed cuneiform writing, one of the oldest forms of writing. Through their studies, the Babylonians made discoveries that changed the way the world worked.

Babylonian maths, for example, was extremely advanced for its time. They were the first to introduce the concept of sexagesimal numbers (base 60), which gave rise to the division of hours into 60 minutes and minutes into 60 seconds - something we still use today! And it wasn't just maths that flourished. Babylon was one of the main centres for the study of astronomy. *By carefully observing the night sky, they created an accurate lunar calendar and mapped the phases of the moon*, something that helped regulate agriculture and religious festivals.

These innovations didn't happen by chance. There was a culture of continuous learning in Babylon, where knowledge was passed down from generation to generation. Libraries, such as the famous Library of Ashurbanipal, kept clay tablets with scientific, mathematical and literary records. *For the Babylonians, learning was an investment, and this principle still applies to us today.*

The Creation of the Lunar Calendar

One of the most fascinating curiosities about Babylon is its contribution to the creation of the lunar calendar. They realised that by observing the movement of the moon, they could accurately predict natural and seasonal events. *This innovation allowed the Babylonians to better organise their lives, both in agriculture and in religious and social affairs.*

The Babylonian lunar calendar divided the year into twelve lunar months, adjusted from time to time to align with the solar year. This allowed agricultural activities to be synchronised with the seasons, ensuring better harvests and, consequently, more economic stability.

In addition to the calendar, the Babylonians also pioneered the first forms of accounting. *They used clay tablets to record business transactions, something that shaped the way resources were managed.* This rudimentary accounting system was crucial to the development of trade and the economy, and its principles continue to influence resource management to this day.

The Value of Continuous Learning

The biggest lesson we can learn from Babylon is the value of continuous learning. Innovation never stops, and just like the Babylonians, we should always be looking for ways to learn and grow.

Think of your life as a constant process of evolution. The knowledge you acquire today can shape your future, just as the knowledge acquired by the Babylonians influenced entire generations. The world is constantly changing, and those who dedicate themselves to continuous learning are the ones who thrive.

In your personal or professional life, *identifying an area of expertise to deepen or innovate* in can be the difference between staying stagnant or growing. Continuous learning doesn't have to be complicated. It can be as simple as reading a book, watching a documentary or taking an online course. The important thing is to remain curious and willing to learn.

Practical Exercise: Identify an Area of Expertise

Now is the time to apply what we learnt from Babylon. Follow the steps below to identify an area in which you can deepen or innovate and create a study or development plan:

1. **Choose an area of interest**
   Think of an area of your life or career that you would

like to improve or explore more deeply. It could be something related to your work, such as learning a new technical skill, or something personal, such as developing artistic or manual skills. *Remember that knowledge has the power to transform your reality, just as it transformed Babylon.*

2. **Define a learning objective**
Set a clear goal for what you want to achieve. If you're learning something new for your career, perhaps your goal is to improve your performance at work or qualify for a promotion. If it's something personal, your goal may simply be the satisfaction of mastering a new skill or piece of knowledge. *Having a clear goal keeps you focussed and motivated.*

3. **Create a study plan**
Organise the time and resources you need to achieve your goal. You may need to set aside 30 minutes a day to read up on the subject or find courses and support materials. *The important thing is to have a clear and realistic plan that fits into your day-to-day life.* Just as the Babylonians needed to plan their astronomical observations and mathematical calculations, you also need discipline to keep learning.

4. **Apply the knowledge you acquire**
Learning without applying it is like accumulating wealth without spending it. Use what you learn in your day-to-day life. If you're learning something for work, try to apply your new knowledge immediately. If it's a personal skill, find ways to practise it regularly. *The Babylonians not only studied the movement of the stars, but applied this knowledge to organise their lives and the economy of their society.*

5. **Review and adjust your plan as necessary**
Just like any project, your learning plan may need

adjusting. Sometimes the pace may be too fast or too slow, or you may find that the area you've chosen isn't exactly what you imagined. *Be flexible and willing to adjust your path, but stay firm in your resolve to keep learning.*

Babylon and Knowledge: A Lasting Lesson

If there's one thing we can learn from Babylon, it's that knowledge is the most powerful resource a civilisation - or a person - can possess. The Babylonians stood out because they invested in education, science and innovation. *They knew that the world was always changing, and that the secret to survival and success was the ability to adapt and evolve with it.*

Today, we live in a world that is changing even faster. But the principle remains the same: those who seek to learn, grow and innovate are the ones who prosper. *You have the ability to transform your life and your reality, just as the Babylonians transformed theirs, through knowledge.*

So, what will your next area of study be? What innovation will you bring to your life?

CHAPTER 4: LEADERSHIP AND GOVERNANCE - THE CODE OF HAMMURABI AND JUSTICE

"A society only truly prospers when justice is its foundation, and the leader governs with equity."

Looking back at history, one of Babylon's most impressive achievements was the creation of a legal system that served as the basis not only for the governance of its society, but for human civilisation as a whole. The Code of Hammurabi, one of the first codifications of laws in history, is a classic example of how justice and governance can shape the destiny of a nation. *It is more than a set of laws written in stone; it is a representation of just leadership, a guide on how a ruler can balance power, justice and social welfare.*

By studying the Code of Hammurabi, we learn profound lessons about leadership, justice and how these two qualities, when applied well, can guarantee the stability and progress of any society - whether it's an ancient nation like Babylon or a modern organisation today.

The Code of Hammurabi: The Basis of Justice

Created around 1754 BC, the Code of Hammurabi was one of the first attempts to formalise a system of laws. It consisted of 282 articles covering a wide range of aspects of everyday life: commercial disputes, family matters, personal injury and much more. *These laws ensured that everyone, regardless of their social position, knew clearly what their rights and duties were.*

The great merit of the Code of Hammurabi was its ability to create a basis for justice in a society where inequalities were great. *While many legal systems today still seek to guarantee this equality, Hammurabi already understood that strong leadership needed to be balanced by a fair system.* Laws were applied to everyone, from nobles to slaves, bringing a sense of order and predictability, so necessary for a civilisation to flourish.

Interestingly, *the Code of Hammurabi not only controlled social behaviour, but also protected trade*, one of the pillars of the Babylonian economy. Detailed laws on commercial transactions, loans and guarantees served to encourage economic development and minimise risks. By creating a stable and predictable environment for negotiations, the code encouraged the expansion of business and the flow of goods, something fundamental to Babylon's growth as one of the main economic centres of antiquity.

Fair and Effective Leadership

At the heart of the Code of Hammurabi is the idea of just leadership. *Hammurabi understood that effective leadership was not just about strength or power, but about ensuring that decisions were made on the basis of principles of justice and fairness.* He knew that his governance would only be respected and effective if it was perceived as fair by his subjects.

The concept of "an eye for an eye, a tooth for a tooth", which became famous in this code, is often misinterpreted. Rather than representing revenge, the principle signified an attempt to propose a punishment proportionate to the crime, *which at the time was a notable advance on the arbitrary justice that used to prevail in ancient societies.* This helped maintain social order while limiting punitive excesses.

Applying this concept to the present day, *a good leader is one who makes decisions based on principles of fairness, who considers the circumstances of each individual and doesn't just blindly impose rules.* In a professional or personal context, this means treating people impartially, listening to all parties involved and ensuring that justice is done in a balanced way.

Curiosity: Laws That Protect Commerce

One of the great curiosities of the Code of Hammurabi was the extent to which it reflected the importance of commerce and the economy in Babylonia. Many of the laws were aimed at protecting economic transactions, ensuring that contracts were respected and that trade could thrive in an environment of trust. For example, there were specific laws on loans, guarantees and even the liability of boatmen who transported goods across the Euphrates. *These commercial regulations were essential to maintain the flow of goods and services that sustained the Babylonian economy.*

Today, the legacy of these laws can be seen in our modern systems of contract and commercial law, where transparency and the fulfilment of agreements are fundamental to economic success. The application of these laws encouraged the development of a solid and reliable commercial network, which allowed Babylon to grow and prosper.

Practical Lesson: Fair and Effective Leadership

Like Hammurabi, you too can apply principles of justice and fairness in your personal and professional life. *Fair leadership inspires respect and trust, two essential elements for the success of any team or organisation.*

Steps towards fair and effective leadership:

1. **Listen to all parties involved:**
   When you are in a leadership position, whether at home, at work or in an organisation, it is crucial that you listen to everyone involved before making a decision. *A fair leader considers all sides of the story before acting.*

2. **Be transparent in your decisions:**
   Just as the Code of Hammurabi was clear and accessible to everyone, your decisions as a leader must also be transparent. Explain your reasons for taking certain actions and ensure that everyone understands the criteria by which you made your decisions.

3. **Apply justice proportionately:**
   In the Code of Hammurabi, punishments were proportionate to the crimes committed. In the same way, *your responses to the actions of others should be balanced and fair*, taking into account the specific situation and the impact of the actions. Don't go overboard with punishments, but don't be too lenient with harmful behaviour either.

4. **Promote an environment of trust:**
   Fair leadership creates an environment of trust, where people feel safe to express their opinions and concerns. This not only improves the organisational climate, but also increases productivity and overall satisfaction.

5. **Be consistent in your actions:**
   Consistency is one of the hallmarks of fair leadership. *By acting in a predictable and coherent way, you establish a standard of justice that everyone can trust.* This doesn't mean that you can't be flexible, but that your principles of justice must be clear and applied in a balanced way in all situations.

Practical Exercise: Applying Principles of Justice and Ethics

Now is the time for you to put Hammurabi's teachings into

practice. Think of a recent leadership situation in your life - it could be something to do with work, family or a personal project. Use the steps below to apply principles of justice and fairness to that situation:

1. **Reflect on the situation:**
   What was the problem or challenge you faced? Was there a difficult decision to be made? Make an honest analysis of the situation and what you could have done differently.

2. **Listen to those involved:**
   Think about how you dealt with the people involved. Did you listen to all sides before making a decision? If not, how could you have done it more fairly? *Remember that listening is one of the greatest tools of effective leadership.*

3. **Evaluate your decision:**
   Was your decision proportionate to the problem? Were you fair in your response? Reflect on whether your action was balanced and considered all the variables. *Applying justice in a proportionate way is essential to earning the respect of those you lead.*

4. **Improve your leadership process:**
   Think about how you can apply these principles more effectively in the future. What adjustments would you make to ensure that your decisions are always fair and balanced?

Justice as the Basis for Prosperity

The Code of Hammurabi teaches us that justice is the basis for a prosperous society. *In the same way, fair and effective leadership is the foundation for success in any area of life.* By applying principles of fairness, transparency and proportionality in your actions, you create an environment of trust and respect where everyone can thrive.

Whether you're a team leader or someone looking to lead your own life more responsibly, *the principles of justice and ethics inspired by ancient Babylon can help you become more effective, respected and, above all, fair.*

CHAPTER 5: THE ROLE OF RELIGION AND SPIRITUALITY IN BABYLON

"The true strength of a civilisation lies not only in its material achievements, but in the power of its faith and spirituality."

In Babylon, one of the greatest civilisations of antiquity, religion was not just an isolated aspect of life, but a driving force that permeated every decision, every building and every aspect of society. Political power was deeply intertwined with religion, and Babylonian deities were seen as divine guides, influencing everything from the way kings ruled to the daily routines of ordinary people.

The great Etemenanki ziggurat, often associated with the legendary Tower of Babel, is a symbol of how much spirituality was at the heart of this civilisation. *This colossal tower represented a connection between heaven and earth, a bridge between the human world and the divine, showing how fundamental faith was in the daily lives of the Babylonians.*

In this chapter, we'll explore how religion and spirituality shaped Babylon, and how these teachings can be applied to our modern daily lives. We'll see how to balance spirituality with the practical needs of life, creating a routine that combines faith, action and personal values.

Religion and Society: The Basis of Power in Babylon

In Babylon, religion and political power were inseparable. Kings didn't just rule by their military prowess or the wealth of their kingdoms, but also by divine approval. *The Babylonian gods were the supreme authority*, and kings were considered representatives of these gods on earth. This intertwining of spiritual and temporal power provided a solid basis for the governance and stability of society.

Each city had its own protective deity, and the temples, especially the ziggurats, were the centres of religious life. *Priests played a fundamental role, not only as spiritual leaders, but also as political and economic counsellors.* They interpreted the signs of the gods, guiding the rulers in their decisions and helping to maintain social order.

A fascinating example is the cult of Marduk, Babylon's main god. Marduk was elevated to the status of supreme god during Hammurabi's reign, and this solidified the unity of the empire. By associating his power with that of Marduk, Hammurabi was able to legitimise his authority over various city-states and peoples.

But the influence of religion didn't stop there. It also guided society's rules of coexistence, customs and moral values. *Laws were seen as an extension of the will of the gods*, and following these laws was a way of maintaining harmony between the human and divine worlds. This shows us how faith can serve as a powerful ethical guide for everyday practical decisions.

Curiosity: The Etemenanki Ziggurat and the Tower of Babel

One of the great curiosities about Babylon is the construction of the Etemenanki ziggurat, a monumental tower that many historians believe was the inspiration for the famous biblical story of the Tower of Babel. *Etemenanki, which means "The House of the Foundation of Heaven and Earth," was an impressive structure dedicated to the god Marduk*, and represented the Babylonians' attempt to connect with the divine. Its height and grandeur symbolised human ambition to reach heaven, while its destruction, according to the biblical narrative, reflects the limitation and fallibility of that ambition.

This story, regardless of its literal veracity, brings us an important lesson: the balance between the spiritual and the material. *While we seek greatness in our lives, we need to remember that true elevation comes from balance and humility before the divine.* Just as Etemenanki sought to touch the sky, our spirituality must elevate us, but always with awareness and moderation.

The Role of Priests

Babylonian priests played a central role in both the spiritual life and the practical organisation of society. *They were not only religious leaders, but also scholars, astronomers and mathematicians.* The priests were responsible for maintaining the lunar calendar, which was essential for agriculture and religious festivities. In addition, they played a key role in coronation ceremonies, where the king received the divine blessing to rule.

The figure of the priest, then, was much more than just a spiritual leader; he was an intermediary between the gods and men, *someone who possessed both practical knowledge and spiritual wisdom.* This duality is an example of how we can, today, seek this balance between spirituality and the practical needs of life.

Practical Lesson: Balancing Spirituality and Practice

Spirituality, in its deepest sense, is not an escape from reality, but a way of living each moment with more clarity, purpose and meaning. We often think of spirituality as something separate from everyday life - something reserved for moments of prayer, meditation or the rituals we practise on certain days. However, when truly understood, *spirituality permeates everything we do, from the simplest interactions to the most complex decisions.* It can serve as an internal compass, guiding our choices based on high principles such as compassion, honesty and gratitude.

When we look at ancient Babylon, we see a society where religion and practical life were deeply intertwined. *The Babylonians didn't see spirituality as something separate from their daily activities.* On the contrary, they believed that their gods were directly involved in every aspect of life - from the planting of crops to the way they conducted their business. This integration of faith and practice was essential to the success and stability of Babylonian society. We can learn a lot from this approach and apply it to our own modern lives.

Let's now explore concrete steps to balance spirituality and practice, bringing a greater sense of purpose and clarity to your daily actions.

Steps to Integrate Spirituality and Practice into Your Daily Life

1. identify your core spiritual values

The first step to integrating spirituality and practice is to understand what really guides your life. *What are the core spiritual values that define who you are and how you want to live?* These values can be based on your faith, religious beliefs, philosophy of life or simply what you feel is most important.

For example, *compassion* may be a core spiritual value. If so, you may wish to practise kindness and empathy in your daily interactions, helping others and being patient with their failings and difficulties. *Gratitude* can also be a core value - the daily practice of recognising the blessings, big and small, in your life.

Pause and ask yourself: Which values resonate most deeply with you? These values will serve as the foundation on which you will build your daily actions. Write down at least three spiritual values that you want to cultivate. Remember, these values don't have to be perfect, but they must be authentic to you.

"When we identify our spiritual values, we begin to live with

intention, guided by what we believe to be right and true."

2. Create a Spiritual Routine

Now that you're clear about the values you want to cultivate, the next step is to create a spiritual routine that helps you connect with these values on a regular basis. *It doesn't have to be elaborate; simplicity is often more powerful and effective.*

For example, if you value compassion, you could take a few minutes every morning to reflect on how you can be more compassionate throughout the day. It could be as simple as offering a word of encouragement to someone or practising patience in a difficult situation.

If gratitude is an important value for you, take a few minutes in the evening to reflect on the things you are grateful for. This helps you maintain a positive outlook and connect with life's blessings, even in difficult times.

Other spiritual practices include meditation, prayer, reading sacred texts or simply being in silence, reflecting on the day. The key is that your spiritual practice *is personal and meaningful*, connecting you with your values and helping to bring clarity and purpose to your daily activities.

"Spiritual practice is not an isolated act, but a thread that intertwines with all our actions, connecting who we are with what we do."

3. Act on Your Values

Spirituality isn't just about introspection; it's about *action*. Spirituality should guide your daily choices and behaviour, not just in big decisions, but in the small interactions and challenges you face.

When faced with a difficult choice or a tense moment, ask yourself: *"How can I act according to my spiritual values in this situation?"* This can be especially useful in times of stress, when it's easy to react impulsively.

For example, if patience is one of your values, instead of reacting with frustration to a challenging person or situation, try taking a deep breath and choosing a calmer, more understanding response. If honesty is a core value, you might strive to be more transparent in your communications, even when it's uncomfortable.

This process of applying your spiritual values to your daily actions can *completely transform the way you interact with the world*, helping you to live in a way that is more in line with who you really are.

"Every action is an opportunity to express our spiritual values, creating a life that reflects what is truest in us."

4. Practise Gratitude

Gratitude is a powerful spiritual practice that can transform your perspective and bring more joy and clarity to your life. We are often so focused on the difficulties and challenges we face that we forget to recognise the many blessings around us.

Take a moment at the end of each day to reflect on what was positive. It could be something as simple as a smile from a friend, a tasty meal or overcoming a challenge. This practice of gratitude helps you maintain a constant connection with what is essential and divine, reminding you that even in the most difficult times, there is always something to be grateful for.

Gratitude roots us in the present and connects us with the abundance that already exists in our lives. By practising it regularly, we begin to see life in a new light, recognising that spirituality is present in every aspect of existence.

"The practice of gratitude is a daily reminder that, even in difficulties, we are blessed in many ways."

5. Review and Adjust Your Routine

Just as the Babylonian priests adjusted the lunar calendar to ensure that festivities and harvests took place at the right time, *you too should adjust your spiritual routine as necessary.* Life is dynamic and constantly changing, as are your needs and circumstances.

Reflect regularly on your spiritual routine and ask yourself: *"Is this practice still working for me? Do I feel connected to my values? Do I need to adjust anything to better align my life with my spirituality?"*

You may realise that you need more time for reflection or, on the contrary, you may be ready to incorporate more concrete actions into your spiritual practice. The important thing is to be flexible and recognise that *spirituality is not static*; it must grow and evolve with you.

"Just as the moon changes its phases, our spirituality must adjust to the new realities of life, always guiding us towards what is true and essential."

Practical Exercise: Creating a Spiritual Routine

Now it's your turn to create a spiritual routine that helps you integrate faith and action into your daily life. Follow the steps below to get started:

1. Define Your Personal Values

What are the most important spiritual values for you? *Write down at least three values that will serve as your guide in all areas of life.* These values are the foundation on which you will build your spiritual routine.

2. Choose a Spiritual Practice

Choose a daily or weekly practice that connects you with these values. *It could be something as simple as five minutes of meditation in the morning, or a more formal practice*, such as attending a temple or church regularly.

3. Integrate Your Values into Your Daily Actions

Think about how you can apply these values in your daily life. *For example, if patience is an important value for you, how can you practise it in stressful situations at work or at home?*

4. Reflect at the End of the Day

Take a moment at the end of each day to reflect on your actions. *Have you managed to live up to your spiritual values? What can you improve tomorrow?*

Remember: spirituality, when practised well, not only connects us to what is highest in us, but also helps us to live more fully, consciously and intentionally.

Spirituality as a Source of Strength

Just as in ancient Babylon, where spirituality permeated every aspect of life, *we too can use our faith and values as a compass to guide our actions in the modern world.* It's not about separating spirituality from practical life, but finding ways to integrate them in a harmonious and meaningful way.

Remember that *true transformation begins from within*, and that by balancing your spirituality with practice, you can reach a deeper level of fulfilment and purpose. Babylon teaches us that faith is not just a belief, but an active force that, when combined with action, can build empires - or, in your case, a full and balanced life.

CHAPTER 6: THE ART OF DIPLOMACY AND FOREIGN RELATIONS

"The true strength of an empire lies not only in its army, but in its ability to build bridges through diplomacy."

This phrase summarises the essence of how Babylon, one of the most powerful empires of antiquity, maintained its influence and prosperity not only through military strength, but also through the strategic intelligence of its diplomatic relations. Diplomacy, more than just a political tool, was an *essential means of guaranteeing the empire's stability and progress*, creating alliances, resolving conflicts and keeping trade routes active.

In this chapter, we'll explore the fascinating art of Babylonian diplomacy and how we can apply its lessons to our own lives, in both personal and professional contexts. *After all, the ability to negotiate, build partnerships and resolve conflicts is as valuable today as it was in ancient Babylon.*

The Power of Diplomacy in Babylon

Babylon realised that raw power, no matter how impressive, was *not enough to keep a vast and diverse empire under control*. So while armies ensured order within its borders, diplomacy took care of what lay beyond them. The Babylonian kings were masters at building alliances with other kingdoms and negotiating agreements that benefited both parties.

A notable example is Nebuchadnezzar II, one of Babylon's best-known rulers. Although he was a formidable military leader, *his success in creating a stable and prosperous empire was equally attributed to his skilful diplomacy.* He knew that to ensure peace and prosperity, especially with neighbouring peoples, it was necessary to build relationships of trust, respect local cultures and maintain treaties that ensured mutual benefits.

"Diplomacy is the art of speaking the truth in such a way that everyone can find value in it." The treaties and alliances signed by Babylon often included agreements on the free movement of goods, guarantees of military support and even marriages between royal families, ensuring that economic and social interests were mutually protected. This ensured that the trade routes, which were vital to the empire's prosperity, remained open and secure.

Curiosity: Diplomacy to Control Distant Territories

A fascinating curiosity is how Babylon used diplomacy to *maintain control over distant territories without the need for constant military intervention.* Instead of relying exclusively on force, the Babylonian kings established local governors who had the task of maintaining peace and order, while maintaining close ties with Babylon through diplomatic agreements and treaties. This allowed Babylon to rule vast regions with relative stability, without the wear and tear of a constant military presence in each territory.

This approach teaches us something important: *true influence doesn't have to be imposed by force*, but can be maintained through trust, mutual respect and co-operation.

Practical Lesson: The Power of Negotiation and Building Healthy Relationships

Just as Babylon flourished by combining strength with diplomacy, we can also learn the importance of *negotiating and building healthy relationships in our own lives.* Whether at work, in friendships or in family relationships, the ability to resolve conflicts and strengthen partnerships is crucial to success.

Here are some practical steps to apply Babylonian diplomacy techniques in your daily life:

1. Understand the Other Person's Point of View

Before starting any negotiation or resolving a conflict, it is essential to understand the other person's point of view. *Empathy is the key to successful diplomacy.* Try to see the situation through the other person's eyes, understanding their concerns, motivations and expectations. This creates a space of mutual respect, where both parties feel heard and valued.

In the professional context, for example, when negotiating a contract or a partnership, consider the interests of the other party and look for points of intersection between your objectives and theirs. *Remember: a successful negotiation is not about winning, but about creating a win-win solution.*

2. Seek Mutual Benefit

In Babylonian diplomacy, treaties generally offered benefits to both sides. Similarly, in our negotiations, we should always look for a solution that is advantageous to all parties involved. Instead of adopting a competitive approach, try to *build bridges* and find a middle ground where everyone wins.

For example, in a workplace conflict, instead of focussing on who is right or wrong, try to identify solutions that meet the needs of everyone involved. This not only solves the current problem, but strengthens relationships for the future.

3. Stay Calm and Respectful

Diplomacy requires *calm, patience and respect.* During difficult negotiations or moments of conflict, it's easy to let emotions take over. However, a calm and respectful attitude is essential to keep the dialogue open and productive. Babylon understood that mutual respect was fundamental to maintaining peace and prosperity.

When dealing with challenging situations, whether at home or at work, take a deep breath and focus on the solution, not the problem. *Respect builds trust*, and trust is the foundation of any successful relationship.

4. Use Effective Communication

Babylonian diplomacy depended on *clear and effective communication*. Messages between kings and governors were carefully worded to avoid misunderstandings and ensure that all terms were well understood. In the same way, it is crucial that you communicate your intentions, expectations and desires clearly when negotiating or resolving conflicts.

When communicating, *be direct but kind*. Use language that is easy to understand and that shows respect for the other side. Make sure that both parties are on the same page and that any agreement is mutually understood.

5. Build long-term relationships

Babylonian diplomacy was not about quick fixes or temporary solutions. It was about building lasting alliances that would guarantee long-term stability. Similarly, when applying diplomacy techniques in your personal or professional life, *think long-term*.

Build relationships that are based on trust, respect and mutual benefit. Investing in healthy relationships today will ensure that in the future you have reliable allies by your side, whether in times of success or difficulty.

Practical Exercise: Applying Diplomacy Techniques

Now that we understand the value and relevance of diplomacy, not only as a historical mechanism used by empires such as Babylon, but also as a fundamental tool for our everyday lives, it's time to apply these ideas. Below, we detail an exercise that can help you implement diplomacy techniques in real situations you face, whether at work, in personal relationships or in any other context where the ability to negotiate and build alliances is essential.

1. identify a conflict situation or partnership opportunity

The first step is to identify a real situation in your life where there is a conflict to be resolved or an opportunity to build a partnership. Think of a situation that requires an effort of communication and negotiation to resolve.

For example, you may be facing a disagreement with a work colleague over the division of responsibilities on a project. Perhaps you're dealing with a difference of opinion at home, or maybe you're negotiating a new contract with a client. Or there may be a partnership opportunity in your circle of friends or community that you want to strengthen.

Choose a situation that is important to you and has real implications for your life. The more significant the issue, the more you will realise the benefits of applying the principles of diplomacy. *Identifying a real situation is the first step to start practising these skills effectively.*

2. Understand the Other Person's Point of View

Successful diplomacy always starts with empathy. Before trying to resolve a conflict or strengthen a partnership, you need to deeply understand what the other person or party involved wants and what they are trying to achieve. This means not just listening, but really *understanding* their point of view.

Take time to reflect on the motivations, interests and concerns of the other party. Ask questions like:

- What are this person's objectives?
- What's at stake for her?
- What are your worries or fears?
- What would she like to get out of this situation?

For example, if you're dealing with a conflict at work, try to understand what's worrying your colleague. Perhaps they are feeling overloaded or have concerns about the visibility of their work. In the case of a contract negotiation, the client may be concerned about costs or on-time delivery. *Understanding what drives the other person is the first step towards creating a solution that is beneficial to both parties.*

3. Seek Mutual Benefit

One of the great lessons of Babylonian diplomacy was that, in many situations, there is no such thing as a "winner" and a "loser". Instead, the focus is on *finding a win-win solution*. This doesn't mean that everyone will get exactly what they want, but rather that the solutions seek to fulfil, at least partially, the interests of everyone involved.

Now that you understand the other party's desires and motivations, think about how you can structure a solution that meets both your needs and theirs. What compromises might you be willing to make? What concessions can you offer to reach an agreement that is satisfactory for everyone?

For example, in the event of a disagreement with a work colleague, perhaps you could suggest a more balanced division of labour or propose a meeting to openly discuss everyone's responsibilities. In a contract negotiation, you can offer flexible deadlines or a discount to the client, provided they commit to a greater volume of services.

The key is to remember that effective diplomacy seeks mutual benefit, not unilateral victory. Negotiations that meet the needs of both sides have a greater chance of success and also strengthen the relationship between the parties.

4. Communicate clearly

Communication is the central tool of any diplomat. It is through effective communication that solutions are presented and negotiations take place. When the time comes to meet or talk to the other party, be prepared to be clear and direct, but *always remain respectful and calm.*

Here are some tips for communicating diplomatically:

- **Be clear about your intentions:** Explain transparently what you want to achieve, without beating around the bush. This avoids misunderstandings and creates a climate of trust.
- **Use respectful language:** Even when emotions are running high, maintain an attitude of respect and consideration for the other person. This facilitates dialogue and prevents the conversation from turning into a bigger conflict.
- **Listen carefully:** Listening is a vital part of communication. Give the other person space to express their ideas and concerns, and show that you are genuinely interested in understanding their point of view.
- **Find common ground:** Whenever possible, emphasise the aspects on which you and the other party agree. This helps create a climate of co-operation and makes it easier to negotiate the more difficult points.

For example, during a conversation with your work colleague, explain that you want to find a solution that works well for both of you and that you are willing to make adjustments. During a contract negotiation, make it clear that you value the long-term relationship with the client and that you are willing to find a solution that benefits both of you.

Remember: good communication is not just about what you say, but about how you make the other person feel during the conversation.

5. Strengthen Relationships

Finally, good diplomacy doesn't end when an agreement is reached. Just as Babylon used its diplomatic alliances to secure long-term relationships, *you too can use situations of conflict and negotiation as opportunities to strengthen your partnerships and personal relationships.*

Once you have reached a solution, reflect on how you can continue to nurture this relationship in the future. Be proactive in demonstrating that the other party can trust you, and look for ways to keep the communication channel open.

For example, in the workplace, continue to collaborate positively with your colleague even after the conflict has been resolved. In the case of a negotiation with a client, try to maintain an effective after-sales relationship by sending updates and showing that you value the long-term partnership.

Strengthening relationships means building trust and demonstrating that the partnership goes beyond a momentary agreement. Healthy, lasting relationships create a network of support and co-operation that will be valuable in many other areas of your life.

Just as Babylon ensured its prosperity through the art of diplomacy, you too can apply these lessons to resolve conflicts, strengthen relationships and build lasting alliances. *True strength lies not in the imposition of power, but in the ability to create harmony and co-operation.* By practising these techniques, you'll see that the key to success often lies not in brute force, but in building bridges that connect people and their interests.

CHAPTER 7: LEGACY AND FALL - THE LESSONS OF BABYLON'S DECLINE

"Great empires do not fall because of a single mistake, but because of a succession of overlooked failures." Babylon, one of the most powerful and influential civilisations of antiquity, was not immune to this. Its meteoric rise was as impressive as its inevitable decline. History teaches us that behind every great fall there are valuable lessons for those willing to learn. In this chapter, we will explore the legacy and fall of Babylon and draw lessons that can be applied directly to our personal and professional lives.

The Decline of the Empire: Strategic Mistakes and Persian Invasions

Babylon was a classic example of how an apparently invincible empire can crumble when its foundations begin to crack. For centuries, the Babylonians built a civilisation marked by cultural, economic and diplomatic advances. However, their downfall was not caused by a single factor, but by a series of strategic errors that accumulated.

The last kings of Babylon, especially Nabonidus, began to distance themselves from the needs of their people and the values that had sustained the empire. The lack of connection with the main Babylonian deities and the prioritisation of personal and religious interests over the management of the empire weakened the social and political foundations. *This disconnection between the leaders and the people opened up gaps that other empires, such as the Persian, were able to capitalise on.*

Historical curiosity

The fall of Babylon, especially its conquest by Cyrus the Great, is one of the most fascinating historical events of antiquity, and the way it happened reveals a lot about the inner workings of empires and the factors that contribute to their collapse.

Cyrus the Great was the founder of the Achaemenid (Persian) Empire, and his approach to the conquest of Babylon in 539 BC highlights his unique strategic ability. Unlike many conquerors of the time, who destroyed the cities they captured as a show of power, Cyrus opted for a path of diplomacy and political psychology, something unusual for the period.

Babylon's Internal Dissatisfaction

In the years leading up to the fall of Babylon, the empire was weakened by internal tensions. Nabonidus, the last Babylonian king, had alienated a large part of the religious elite by distancing himself from the traditional cults that sustained the city's social cohesion. He devoted himself to the cult of Sin, the lunar god, and distanced himself from the celebrations and rituals involving Marduk, the Babylonians' main god. This weakened popular support and, more crucially, the support of the priests, who were a powerful and influential class in Babylon.

With this growing dissatisfaction among the population and the religious elite, Babylon was ripe to be conquered in an unconventional way. Instead of trying to take the city by force, **Cyrus was able to exploit these internal divisions**, presenting himself not as a barbarian invader, but as a liberator. He promised to restore the traditional cults of Marduk and bring back prosperity and order, something that attracted the support of both the priests and the population.

The Peaceful Entry of Cyrus

According to the *Cylinder of Cyrus*, an archaeological artefact that narrates his version of the conquest, Cyrus was welcomed by the priests and the Babylonian population with virtually no resistance. The account suggests that the Babylonian people were so disillusioned with Nabonidus' rule that they preferred to see a new ruler, especially one who respected their religious traditions. *This level of internal co-operation was essential for the peaceful conquest.*

Military and Diplomatic Strategy

From a military point of view, Cyrus was also brilliant. His armies diverted the course of the Euphrates River, which ran through the middle of Babylon, allowing his soldiers to enter the city through an almost dry channel, taking the Babylonian defence by surprise. *This strategy was efficient and avoided a prolonged siege or battles within the walls, preserving the city's infrastructure and people.*

However, Cyrus didn't just rely on his military strength. He had already established alliances with groups inside and outside Babylon, ensuring that when his invasion was launched, there would be as little resistance as possible. By positioning himself as a restorer of order and traditional values, he won the support not only of the religious elite, but also of local and foreign leaders who were dissatisfied with Nabonidus' regime.

The Consequence of the Peaceful Fall

The fall of Babylon under Cyrus was not only a change of leadership, but also a turning point in the way conquests were carried out and perceived. Instead of destroying Babylon and subjugating its people, **Cyrus incorporated the city into his empire without jeopardising its institutions**. He allowed religious services to continue, even restoring temples and returning sacred icons that had been looted by Nabonidus.

Cyrus' success in conquering Babylon without major bloodshed, keeping the power and cultural structures intact, was due to his understanding of the city's **internal dynamics**. He knew that Babylon's real weakness was not in its walls, but in the divisions between its government and its people. *This conquest emphasised that empires often fall more because of their internal failings than because of external threats.*

In addition, **Cyrus was skilful at political propaganda**, using documents such as the Cyrus Cylinder to portray his conquest as a liberation rather than an invasion. He was recognised both by the Babylonians themselves and by other nations as a just and benevolent ruler, which facilitated Babylon's integration into the growing Persian Empire.

Modern Lessons from the Fall of Babylon

This historical narrative has many lessons that we can apply to modern times. The fall of Babylon teaches us that an empire, an organisation or even a personal career can appear strong from the outside, but if there are internal divisions and dissatisfaction, collapse can come from within, often without any external warning. *The true strength of a nation, company or individual lies in internal cohesion, an understanding of its core values and the ability to adapt in the face of challenges.*

The example of Cyrus also shows us that, in many cases, *diplomacy, strategy and understanding the needs of others* can be much more powerful tools than brute force. He conquered Babylon not by destruction, but by restoration - offering the people what they wanted most: a return to tradition and respectful leadership.

Thus, the fall of Babylon reminds us that, **before seeking external conquests, it is essential to ensure that our internal foundation is solid**, whether on a personal or organisational level. Staying connected to our core values, listening to the needs of those around us and adapting to change are the keys to avoiding decline and ensuring a prosperous longevity.

Practical Lesson: Learning from Past Mistakes

Babylon's strategic mistakes are powerful lessons for all of us. Sometimes we find ourselves in situations that seem stable and secure, but if we're not vigilant, cracks can form and lead to avoidable failures. This can happen in our relationships, careers or projects. The key is to **spot the signs** and **correct course** before the decline becomes irreversible.

Here are some lessons we can learn from Babylon's decline:

1. **Disconnection from core values:** Just as the Babylonian leaders distanced themselves from the traditions and divinities that gave meaning to the empire, we often lose our way when we move away from our own core values. *What guides you in your life? What are the values that, if neglected, can crumble your foundation?*

2. **Lack of attention to the needs of others:** The success of a leader - whether personal or professional - depends on their ability to understand and meet the needs of others. When we focus only on our own priorities, as Nabonido did, we lose the trust and support of those around us. *Paying attention to the needs of those around you can be the key to avoiding unexpected downfalls.*

3. **Ignoring the warning signs:** Babylon ignored the signs of weakening. The internal tensions, the discontent of the people and the faltering alliances were clear signs that something needed to change. In our lives, the warning signs also appear - whether it's the fraying of a relationship, a lack of motivation at work or the continual failure of a project. *Ignoring these signs can be fatal; success comes from the ability to identify and correct course before it's too late.*

Practical Exercise: Reflection on Personal and Professional

Mistakes

Now, let's apply these lessons to your own life. This exercise is designed to help you reflect on a personal or professional failure and extract valuable lessons for the future. Learning from past mistakes is the key to avoiding the same pitfalls in the present and future.

Steps for the exercise:

1. **Identify a significant failure:** Think of a recent or long-standing failure, whether in a personal or professional context, that has had an important impact on your life. It could be a mistake in a work project, a relationship that ended badly, or an opportunity you missed. The aim is to choose a situation that still has lessons to offer.

Example: "I lost an important contract because I couldn't meet the agreed deadline."

2. **Analyse the causes:** Reflect on the reasons that led to this failure. Ask yourself: What did I do or fail to do that contributed to this result? What external factors influenced the situation? Is there anything I could have foreseen or avoided?

Example: "I underestimated the time needed for the project and didn't warn the client about possible delays. I also failed to ask for help when I needed it."

3. **Find the lessons:** For each cause you've identified, write down a practical lesson that you can apply in the future. This will help you turn failure into learning.

Example: "In the future, I'll be more transparent about deadlines and limitations, and I'll seek help before the situation becomes critical."

4. **Create an action plan:** Based on the lessons learnt, develop a plan to avoid similar mistakes in the future. What steps can you take to ensure that this failure is not repeated? How can you improve your skills,

communication or planning?

Example: "I'm going to divide large projects into smaller parts, with intermediate deadlines, to make sure I'm on the right track. I'm also going to develop more proactive communication with my clients."

5. **Review periodically: Revisit** this reflection from time to time to ensure that you are applying the lessons learnt. The process of improvement is continuous, and the best way to avoid future failures is to ensure that the lessons of the past are always present.

Babylon's Legacy: Learning from the Past

The fall of Babylon was not just the end of an empire; it was a testimony to how even the greatest civilisations can crumble when mistakes are ignored. The famous conquest by Cyrus the Great was not a defeat by brute force, but by internal weakening. This teaches us that no matter how strong or successful you may seem, the real challenge lies in remaining vigilant and connected to the values that underpin your success.

If Babylon had learnt from its own mistakes earlier, its fate might have been different. In the same way, if we learn from our failures and make the necessary adjustments, we can avoid the stumbling blocks that can jeopardise our projects and relationships.

Like Babylon, we all face moments of decline in our lives. However, **true strength lies in recognising these moments, learning from them and turning our mistakes into stepping stones for the future.**

CHAPTER 8: THE SECRET OF BABYLON'S RICHES - MODERN APPLICATIONS

"Babylon's real treasure was not in its golden walls or imposing temples, but in the wisdom that moulded its greatness."

Throughout this book, we explore the most fascinating and instructive aspects of ancient Babylon: its capacity for leadership, its ingenious economic system, its pioneering innovations and its ability to build lasting diplomatic relationships. More than a civilisation that accumulated material wealth, Babylon accumulated **wealth of knowledge** that, surprisingly, resonates in our modern lives. Now it's time to look at these lessons in a new light and discover how we can apply them directly to our daily lives.

Visionary Leadership: The Example of King Hammurabi

Babylonian leadership, especially represented by the famous King Hammurabi, was a combination of firmness and justice. The *Code of Hammurabi*, one of the oldest known systems of laws, not only established clear rules, but also created a sense of order that was essential for maintaining the cohesion of a vast and diverse empire. *The lesson here is simple: leadership is not just about giving orders, but about creating a system in which people can thrive.*

In modern life, the application of this lesson lies in **developing clear and fair structures**, whether in the workplace or in personal relationships. Setting transparent expectations and ensuring that everyone understands their responsibilities creates a sense of security and trust. **Successful companies** such as Google and Microsoft are known for their clear approach to internal governance and organisational culture, where open communication is encouraged and leaders are accessible.

Economy and Innovation: Prosperity as a Result of Intelligent Planning

Babylon was a flourishing economic centre, partly due to its sophisticated system of trade and agriculture. Its innovations in irrigation allowed it to develop a thriving agriculture in a desert environment, showing that **innovation is the key to overcoming limitations**. The intelligent use of available resources ensured that Babylon became the economic heart of the ancient world.

In modern times, the concept of innovation to overcome limitations remains fundamental. *When we look at tech giants like Apple, we see the same innovation mentality that drove Babylon.* Steve Jobs, in presenting the first iPhone, wasn't just creating a new product - he was redefining how we communicate and interact with the world. *Just as the Babylonians adapted the land and water to serve their purposes, we too can use the tools at our disposal to innovate and transform our realities.*

Curiosity: The Role of Banks in Babylon

Interestingly, *Babylon was a pioneer in creating a primitive banking system* that played a crucial role in its economic development and the sophistication of society. Long before modern banks, Babylonian temples and palaces served as financial centres, offering services that we now recognise as fundamental to the functioning of any economy.

These centres were not just places of worship or homes for royalty. In fact, *temples such as that of Marduk, the supreme god of Babylon, and imperial palaces* acted as central financial institutions where wealth was safely stored. These institutions held not only the treasures of kings, but also the assets of ordinary citizens and commercial elites, playing the role of "banks" that stored wealth in the form of precious metals such as gold and silver.

In addition to storing wealth, **Babylon was one of the first places to develop credit practices**. Merchants and citizens could obtain loans from these institutions, with the promise of repayment with interest - another concept that flourished at the time. Contracts were recorded on clay tablets, and both capital and interest were calculated based on specific criteria, showing the mathematical and economic advancement of civilisation.

Imagine you were a Babylonian merchant. You could deposit your surplus grain in a temple and, in return, receive a "credit note", a promise that, within a certain period, you could withdraw the amount or even borrow more grain, paying a small additional percentage. These commercial contracts were among the first signs that the concept of "money" transcended the physical exchange of goods and already entered the territory of **financial promises**, establishing trust between parties.

Another fascinating aspect of the Babylonian banking system was the *introduction of rudimentary insurance*. When shipping goods on long trade routes, the Babylonians could take out a type of "insurance" to protect their cargo. If the goods were lost or stolen during the journey, the merchant would be entitled to compensation, based on terms agreed in advance. This concept of risk mitigation helped to expand trade, providing security and encouraging merchants to explore new routes, even if they were dangerous.

This innovation didn't stop there. The Babylonian government also played a regulatory role, ensuring that these financial practices followed certain rules and protecting the interests of both creditors and debtors. The laws of the *Code of Hammurabi*, for example, included clear rules on interest rates and loan contracts, demonstrating a concern for financial justice and avoiding abuses, something we can consider a primitive form of banking regulation.

Compared to the modern financial system, we can see the roots of many practices that we still use today. The concepts of credit, interest, insurance and regulation already existed in an organised and controlled form thousands of years ago in Babylon. The use of these tools allowed wealth to circulate more efficiently, boosting the economic development of the region and **allowing Babylon to become one of the largest commercial centres in antiquity**.

Today, **credit remains one of the pillars of the global economy**, both for large corporations and small entrepreneurs. Modern banks, brokerages and financial institutions follow practices that were born in Babylonian lands, such as financing projects and offering loans. An important lesson that Babylon teaches us is the importance of **using credit wisely** and understanding the risks and benefits of each financial action.

In order to prosper, it is essential to learn how to apply financial tools such as credit, interest and insurance strategically. Just as the Babylonians did, we must **carefully plan our investments and manage risks responsibly**. Financial success is often not just about accumulating wealth, but about being able to use these tools to grow capital and protect our assets.

The modern application of these lessons can be seen in several current examples. When a company launches a new product, it often resorts to loans or venture capital investments to finance production and marketing. This upfront capital is used strategically to generate future profits, just as the Babylonian merchants used credit to expand their business. And just as the Babylonians protected their cargo with insurance, today modern companies secure their investments with sophisticated insurance policies to minimise losses and protect their assets.

Finally, **the main lesson we can learn from the Babylonian banking system** is that financial progress depends not only on accumulating wealth, but on how we use and protect that wealth. Sustainable financial success is achieved through informed strategic decisions, and Babylonian wisdom teaches us that by planning carefully and using available financial resources intelligently, we can guarantee long-term prosperity.

Babylon reminds us that true wealth goes beyond gold and silver. It lies in our ability to use knowledge to maximise our resources, manage risks and, above all, ensure that our financial legacy is solid and long-lasting.

Diplomacy and Relationships: The Art of Building Bridges

The Babylonians' diplomatic skills were one of the key factors in their survival and prosperity. As we have seen in previous chapters, *Cyrus the Great conquered Babylon not by force, but by diplomatic intelligence.* The empire used alliances, treaties and negotiations to keep territories and trade routes secure, which allowed them to continue to flourish while other civilisations around them fell.

In modern life, the art of diplomacy is equally crucial, whether in the corporate environment or in our personal relationships. Successful negotiations depend on understanding the wishes and motivations of the other party and being able to find solutions that benefit both sides. *At work, knowing how to build bridges between departments or companies can be the key to long-term success.* At home, **cultivating healthy and harmonious relationships** is essential for well-being and lasting happiness.

Practical Lesson: Turning Knowledge into Action

Now that we've revisited Babylon's most powerful lessons, **how can we apply them in our practical lives?** The key to success lies in turning this knowledge into tangible actions, drawing up a strategic plan that can be implemented in our personal or professional projects. Here's a practical guide to help you get started on this journey:

1. **Define Your Objectives Clearly** *The first step to any successful project is to be clear about what you want to achieve.* Define your goals in a specific and measurable way. Think about which areas of your life - be it career, relationships or finances - you want to apply these lessons from Babylon.

2. **Establish Structures and Rules** Just as the *Code of Hammurabi* created a system of order in Babylon, it's important to establish your own structures. What are the "laws" that will guide your actions? *These can be productivity rules, work ethics, or leadership principles.* Make sure these structures support your goals and facilitate progress.

3. **Plan Your Time and Resources** Babylon's success in agriculture and trade was largely due to the **efficient management of available resources**. In the same way, you need to plan how you will use your time and resources (financial, emotional, etc.). Allocating these resources strategically will ensure that your projects not only get off the ground, but are sustained over time.

4. **Implement innovation** Don't be afraid to innovate. Babylon prospered because its leaders and citizens were willing to experiment with new technologies and methods. *In your life, this could mean adopting new tools, techniques or approaches to solve old problems.* Be open to change and always look for ways to improve your operations.

5. **Build Healthy Relationships Diplomacy was essential to the success of Babylon**, and the same goes for your life. Strengthen your relationships, whether at home or at work. Learn to negotiate so that everyone wins, and create alliances that can support you in your goals.

6. **Evaluate and Adjust Your Plan** No plan is perfect from the start. *Just as the Babylonians adapted their strategies over time, you too must be willing to adjust your plan as you go along.* Evaluate your results periodically and be willing to correct course when necessary.

Final Exercise: Creating Your Strategic Plan

To close this chapter and this book, here's a final exercise to help you turn what you've learnt into a concrete strategic plan:

1. **Choose a Main Project or Goal** Think of a goal you want to achieve in the next six months. It could be something related to your work, your personal life or a long-term project.

2. **Write down your structures and rules** Establish the rules that will guide you towards this goal. These should be clear and practical, helping you to stay focused.

3. **Develop a timetable** Create a timetable for carrying out the necessary actions. *Divide your goal into small tasks and set realistic deadlines.*

4. **Implement New Techniques** Look for ways to innovate along the way. Think about how you can do things differently to achieve better results.

5. **Build Alliances** Identify the people who can help or support you on your journey. How can you strengthen these relationships to ensure mutual success?

6. **Monitor and Adjust** Establish a system to monitor your progress and adjust your plan as necessary to ensure you keep moving forward.

With this strategic plan in hand, you'll be ready to apply the **eternal lessons of Babylon** and turn your knowledge into practical, effective action. *The wisdom of an ancient civilisation, when applied correctly, can be the key to thriving in the modern world.*

CONCLUSION

The Secrets of Babylon

Throughout history, ancient Babylon has left us a legacy of wisdom and innovation that has spanned centuries and still resonates strongly in our modern times. The grandeur of their achievements, the vision of their leaders and the way they positioned themselves as a centre of prosperity offer us valuable lessons, not just as mere historical reflections, but as principles that we can apply directly to our lives.

Babylon's secret lay in its ability to combine pragmatism with a long-term vision. They knew that greatness wasn't built only on military conquests or grandiose monuments, but on a solid foundation of strategic planning, justice and innovation. It was through the Code of Hammurabi that they consolidated their legal base, ensuring that every citizen understood their place in society and the rules that governed them. This sense of justice and organisation is still an essential pillar for the success of any modern society. Similarly, in our daily lives, understanding the importance of clear and fair rules helps us to build a more balanced and harmonious personal and professional life.

In addition to its legal system, Babylon flourished as a commercial empire due to its strategic location between the Tigris and Euphrates rivers, which allowed it to be a link between East and West. This success was not by chance, but the result of a mentality focused on innovation and a regulated economy. In a world of uncertainty, its ability to create an international trade network and maintain trust between partners was the secret to its economic growth. This is a practical lesson that we can apply in our own professional context: building relationships based on trust and a long-term vision is the key to sustainable growth, whether in business or in our personal relationships.

Another notable aspect was the power of the visionary leadership of kings like Nebuchadnezzar II, who didn't just expand the territory, but also elevated the name of Babylon through major infrastructure works and architectural innovations. His commitment to creating a lasting legacy demonstrates the importance of balancing ambition with a strategic vision. Like Nebuchadnezzar, we all have the power to build our own "empires" when we put focus and purpose into our daily actions. Whether in our careers or personal lives, long-term vision combined with immediate action is what really allows us to achieve great things.

But perhaps one of the most profound lessons Babylon offers us is about the role of knowledge and persistence. Amid the adversities of their desert environment, the Babylonians were able to innovate in areas such as maths and astronomy, developing tools that would influence future generations. They didn't see challenges as insurmountable barriers, but as opportunities for growth and development. In modern life, this spirit of persistence and the relentless pursuit of knowledge are fundamental to success. Just as Babylon found ways to thrive in adverse conditions, we can learn to look at our personal and professional challenges as opportunities to learn, grow and innovate.

However, just as Babylon had its heyday, it also experienced its decline, caused by internal divisions and a leadership disconnected from the needs of its people. This reminds us that success cannot be taken for granted; it must be nurtured with attention, care and constant adaptation. Often, the greatest failures come not from external threats, but from internal negligence. When we forget to pay attention to the signs of wear and tear - whether in relationships, careers or business - we put ourselves at risk. The fall of Babylon is a powerful reminder that true strength lies in the ability to stay connected to core values and the ability to adapt in the face of change.

So the biggest lesson that Babylon offers us is that success and prosperity are built on a solid foundation of values, planning and innovation, but that in order to sustain this foundation you need to be attentive to people's needs and to the signs of change. By combining these elements - vision, persistence, justice and innovation - we can create a prosperous and meaningful future, just as Babylon did in its time.

Now is the time to apply these lessons to our own journey. As the great history of this ancient empire teaches us, we can build something lasting and great in our lives if we have a clear vision, strategic action and a continuous commitment to learning and improvement. Just as Babylon overcame the challenges of its time, we can also overcome our own by building a life of purpose and success.

The power of Babylon is now in your hands. May you use this wisdom to create your own story of greatness!

APPENDIX TO "THE SECRETS OF BABYLON"

Overview: Wisdom, Wealth and Personal Growth

This appendix has been created to offer a practical and straightforward perspective on the main teachings **of "The Secrets of Babylon"**. Below, we address the most essential points in a concise and applicable way, connecting the ancient wisdom of Babylon with the challenges and opportunities of modern life. Our focus will be on showing how this ancient civilisation offers a rich source of teachings for those seeking success, growth and stability.

1. Prosperity in the Lessons of Babylon

Babylon was one of the most prosperous empires of its time, known for its financial organisation, irrigation systems and trade routes. However, the greatest lesson it offers us is that prosperity is not just a question of accumulating wealth, but of how to manage it strategically and sustainably.

In the modern world, this can be applied in various ways:

- **Financial planning:** Just as the Babylonians regulated trade and agriculture through clear laws, it is essential that we create structured financial planning in our lives. Whether it's creating budgets, setting goals or seeking knowledge about investments, the first step to prosperity is organisation.

- **Sustainable investments:** The Babylonians innovated in areas such as irrigation and astronomy, using knowledge to overcome environmental limitations. Today, we can take inspiration from this by investing in areas that bring long-term sustainable returns, such as education, technology or ethical business.

2. The Power of Persistence

Babylon didn't become an empire overnight. Its rise was the result of strategic planning that took the long term into account. In the book, we are reminded that the true strength of a civilisation or a person lies in their ability to persist.

In everyday life, applying this principle is simple:

- **Consistency of effort:** Just as the walls of Babylon were built stone by stone, our projects and dreams must also be built gradually. We mustn't be discouraged by temporary obstacles; instead, we must focus on daily construction, whether in business, studies or our relationships.
- **Resilience:** Just as Nebuchadnezzar faced challenges to turn Babylon into a power, we must be resilient in the face of adversity. The road to success is not linear, but those who persevere reap the rewards in the end.

3. Visionary Leadership and Justice

Hammurabi, one of Babylon's most important kings, is known for the famous **Code of Hammurabi**, one of humanity's first collections of laws. This code not only regulated society, but also established a standard of justice that brought cohesion and stability to the empire.

In our day, these lessons can be applied as follows:

- **Fair leadership:** Whether in leadership positions or in our families, the true leader is the one who creates an environment of fairness and transparency. Just as Hammurabi ensured that his laws were clear and respected, we must be clear in our expectations and firm

in our principles.
- **Responsible governance:** The application of fair rules and ethical leadership are fundamental in both team management and company development. Babylon teaches us that without a fair system, social (or business) cohesion quickly breaks down.

4. Innovation as a Pillar of Success

One of the reasons Babylon prospered was its ability to innovate, whether in the field of science, maths or agriculture. The Babylonians, with their astrological observations and development of irrigation systems, turned limitations into opportunities.

To apply this principle, we can:

- **Perfect our skills:** Never stop learning. Knowledge was one of Babylon's greatest riches, and it is still the key to our success today. Investing in our education and developing new skills makes us more resilient and adaptable to change.
- **Constant innovation:** No matter what field you're in, always look for ways to do what's already being done better. Babylon prospered because it innovated in commerce, agriculture and even government. Today, those who challenge the status quo are the ones who stand out.

5. Diplomacy and Relationship Building

Babylon didn't survive by force alone, but by its ability to build alliances and negotiate effectively. Nebuchadnezzar II, for example, was a leader who knew how to use diplomacy to expand and protect his empire.

The lessons of Babylonian diplomacy can be applied to our lives:

- **Building alliances:** Just as the Babylonians used diplomacy to ensure their prosperity, we must learn the importance of building healthy relationships. At work or at home, collaboration and negotiation are key to achieving common goals.

- **Conflict resolution:** The ability to mediate conflicts and find solutions that satisfy both parties is a powerful tool, whether in the workplace or in personal life. Success often depends on our ability to build bridges, not walls.

FINAL CONSIDERATIONS

Turning Wisdom into Action

Babylon's legacy is not just in its great buildings or the wealth of its kings, but in the set of values they embodied: persistence, innovation, justice and diplomacy. By applying these principles to our lives, we can build a solid foundation for personal and professional success, facing challenges with confidence and long-term vision.

Just as Babylon overcame its difficulties to become one of the greatest civilisations in history, we too can use this ancient wisdom to transform our lives and achieve our goals with determination and purpose. The power to create a new Babylon is now in our hands - and the secret is to act with wisdom and persistence.

www.ingramcontent.com/pod-product-compliance
Lightning Source LLC
Chambersburg PA
CBHW070412230526
45471CB00006B/2775